From

Sylhet to Spitalfields

The Politics of British Bangladeshis in Tower Hamlets
(1982–2016)

MAYAR AKASH

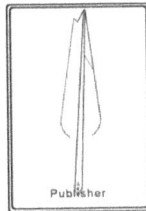

Publisher
MA PUBLISHER

FSC

Paper printed on is FSC Certified, lead free, acid free, buffered paper made from wood-based pulp. Our paper meets the ISO 9706 standard for permanent paper. As such, paper will last several hundred years when stored.

Dedication

To the elders who carried boroughs within them, long before the boroughs carried their names.

To the youth who sat in gallery seats, imagining futures behind microphones and manifestos.

To every Bangladeshi family that stepped onto East London pavements with uncertain footing—and laid down foundations of homes, mosques, businesses, and belonging.

To those who voted, stood, faltered, won, resigned, recontested—and kept showing up.

To the first names on the ballot.

To the hands that opened polling station doors before sunrise.

To the voices told they didn't belong—who answered by standing anyway.

To our parents, who arrived with dreams and dialects.

To our children, who will inherit not just our stories, but our footsteps.

To **Abdul Mukit Chunu MBE, Jainal Abedin, Helal Uddin Abbas, Shabina Aktar, Syed Mizan, Rajon Uddin Jalal, Ayas Miah, Shahid Ali**, and **Mohammed Ali Nanu**, whose lived experiences shaped this book's spine and its heartbeat.

To **Mark Baynes** and **Trial by Jeory**, whose chronicles turned digital pages into mirrors, ensuring Tower Hamlets politics left no truth undocumented.

To Tower Hamlets.

May your alleys, election posters, and arguments always remind us: **representation is never given—it's claimed.**

Preface

This book began not with data, but with a memory: a voter in Whitechapel speaking proudly of a councillor—not because of party or policy, but because "he's from my village in Sylhet." That moment revealed something deeper than electoral politics. It was about belonging, lineage, and representation rooted in migration.

From Sylhet to Spitalfields is a journey—across oceans, wards, and generations. It charts how British Bangladeshis in Tower Hamlets moved from the margins to the ballot box, reshaping not only their borough, but Britain's understanding of civic power. Through councillor lists, ward boundaries, interviews, and statistical patterns, this work attempts to archive what community-led politics sounds like when it's spoken in Sylheti, debated in mosques, and voted in Bethnal Green.

As a researcher, this chronicle taught me that representation is not defined by titles—it's defined by trust. Councillors were not always polished. But they were present. And for many residents, that presence was enough to ignite belief.

This is not a history of perfect heroes. Nor is it a celebration of victory alone. It's a record of attempts—some successful, some fractured—to translate identity into influence.

For those who walked from council estates to campaign offices, for those who knocked on doors before knowing the language, and for those who never saw themselves in the press but saw themselves in the posters—this book is yours.

Acknowledgement

This book was never mine alone.

To the elders who opened doors and stories—your memory is now written into the borough's political archive. To the councillors who allowed me to ask uncomfortable questions and responded with grace, candour, or guarded silence—you taught me that truth has many tones.

To the young volunteers who helped sift through crumpled campaign leaflets, oral interview notes, and council minutes, often working with no promise beyond presence: thank you. Your diligence added structure to stories.

To the community organisations across Spitalfields, Whitechapel, and Shadwell who gave me their trust and tea—your warmth filled pages more than any citation ever could.

To the academics and activists who reviewed early drafts, sharpened arguments, and reminded me to document not just the data but the dignity—your insight runs through every footnote.

To **Abdul Mukit Chunu MBE, Jainal Abedin, Helal Uddin Abbas, Shabina Aktar, Syed Mizan, Rajon Uddin Jalal, Ayas Miah, Shahid Ali,** and **Mohammed Ali Nanu**—thank you for your insight, your candour, and for entrusting me with stories that shaped this archive.

To **Mark Baynes** of www.lovewapping.org and **Trial by Jeory** at www.trialbyjeory.com—your digital chronicles provided a vital compass. Your work tracked what local politics often tried to obscure, especially in mapping the journey of British Bangladeshi councillors.

Finally, to those who stood for election but were never elected: your efforts are here. Your names appear alongside those who won because memory does not distinguish between victory and effort. It remembers both.

This book was written in service of remembering—and in gratitude for being allowed to listen.

Contents

Dedication   3
Preface   5
Acknowledgement   6
Contents   8
Introduction   10
Chapter 1   12
   Taking The Bull By The Horns   12
Chapter 2   14
   From Breakthrough To Legacy   14
Chapter 3   17
   From Local Resolve To National Representation   17
Chapter 4   20
   The Politics Of Belonging   20
Chapter 5   23
   Public Duty Or Political Career?   23
Chapter 6   26
   Discontent And Scrutiny   26
Chapter 7   29
   2010 – Triumph And Turmoil   29
Chapter 8   32
   Community In Motion   32
Chapter 9   35
   Behind The Ballot   35
Chapter 10   38
   Redrawing The Map   38
Chapter 11   41
   Roots And Representation   41
Chapter 12   45
   The Numbers Tell Stories (Polished Version)   45
Chapter 13   48
   Legacy And Learning   48
Glossary   50
Appendices   52
Epilogue: 55
Bibliography   56
   Official Records And Reports   56
   Books And Academic Works   56
   Interviews And Oral Histories   57
   Journalism And Community Media   57
   Web And Digital Sources   58

Sources Consulted 59
Endnotes 59
Synopsis 61

Introduction

This is not simply a study of elections. It is a story of arrival, aspiration, and the long shadow cast by memory.

In 1982, when I first began tracing the steps of British Bangladeshi politics in Tower Hamlets, there were few names on ballots that felt familiar—and even fewer doors open to those who had arrived with dialects, dreams, and no guarantees. What began as quiet presence—community elders attending council meetings or informal gatherings at mosques—grew into loud persistence: campaign posters in Bengali, debates over local schooling, and first-time candidates standing not to win, but to be seen.

This book follows that journey—not from above, but from within. I walked those pavements. I listened in those tea shops. I watched the ward boundaries change, the parties realign, the community realign with them. Through councillor lists, personal interviews, oral histories, and a decade of electoral archives, this work maps how representation was shaped by migration, faith, trust, and friction.

Tower Hamlets is more than a borough. For many, it was a political proving ground. Respect, Labour, Tower Hamlets First, Aspire—these were not just party labels, they were vessels for something deeper: identity, recognition, resistance.

This chronicle is grounded in specificity: the zila connections that defined candidate loyalty, the female pioneers who entered council chambers for the first time, the boundary reforms that redrew allegiances and confused voters. Yet beneath the numbers lies a more intimate truth—that representation, for communities like ours, was never inevitable. It was claimed. Slowly. Fiercely.

This book is written in gratitude to those who stood, and those who stood beside them. May it serve as an archive, a mirror, and a call to memory.

Chapter 1

Taking the Bull by the Horns

Abstract

This chapter explores the initial foray of British Bangladeshis into Tower Hamlets politics, particularly the emergence of community-led representation and the sociocultural motivators behind early candidacies.

Keywords

Tower Hamlets, British Bangladeshis, political participation, representation, electoral history

Introduction

Beginning with the historic election of Md Ashik Ali in 1982, the community's entry into local politics marked a turning point in postcolonial identity assertion. Prior to this, Bangladeshi civic visibility remained marginal, often shaped by cultural organisations rather than elected representation.

Body

- **Political Landscape of the 1980s**
  - Rise in racial tensions post-1971
  - Community mobilisation post-Altab Ali's murder
- **Formation of Identity-Driven Voting Patterns**
  - Spitalfields as the early nucleus
  - First candidates often had no formal educational credentials but strong community recognition
- **Party Dynamics**

- Labour's role in early integration
- Independence from mainstream parties where necessary

"The qualification required for this post is life experience, intelligence... The people do the rest, they vote you in." — *Community interviewee*

Tables

Table 1.1: Elected Councillors (1982)

Year	Ward	Councillor	Party
1982	St Katharine's	Md Ashik Ali	Lab
1982	Spitalfields	Md Nurul Huque	Ind

Discussion

The Bangladeshi community's political entry was both symbolic and tactical. While representation began with individuals like Md Ashik Ali, the subsequent decades would see greater complexity as education, gender, and party politics entered the mix.

Conclusion

This chapter sets the stage for understanding the evolution of political identity among Bangladeshis in East London—not just as voters, but as shapers of policy and public space.

Chapter 2

From Breakthrough to Legacy

Abstract

This chapter explores the emergence and evolution of Bangladeshi female political representation in Tower Hamlets, highlighting pioneering candidates, challenges faced, and the symbolic milestones that reshaped gender dynamics within a traditionally male-dominated diaspora.

Keywords

Gender politics, British Bangladeshis, Tower Hamlets, representation, pioneers

Introduction

The journey of British Bangladeshi women into politics in Tower Hamlets began in earnest with the election of Mrs. Pola Manzila Uddin in 1990. Her success was more than symbolic—it opened doors, redefined expectations, and anchored a new paradigm of civic participation where identity and gender intersected with power.

Body

2.1 Early Participation

- **1990**: Mrs. Uddin elected in Shadwell as the first Bangladeshi female councillor
- Her election marked a transition from cultural presence to institutional power.

"I entered politics to represent voices that were often spoken about but seldom heard." — Interview extract

2.2 Expanding the Field

- Between 1990–2010, a slow but steady increase in female candidates—across Labour, Respect, and Liberal Democrats.
- Candidates like Rabina Khan and Shiria Khatun became known for contesting multiple elections and achieving visible impact.

2.3 Barriers & Breakthroughs

- Challenges included patriarchal norms, party gatekeeping, and media scrutiny.
- Campaigning often required support from community networks otherwise dominated by male activists.

2.4 Statistical Overview

Table 2.1: Bangladeshi Female Candidates (1990–2016)

Year	Ward	First Name	Surname	Party
1990	Shadwell	Pola Manzila	Uddin	Lab
1994	Shadwell	Pola Manzila	Uddin	Lab
1998	St Peter's	Jusna	Begum	Lab
2002	Millwall	Mumtaz	Samad	Lab
2006	Bow West	Anwara	Ali	Lab
2010	Shadwell	Rabina	Khan	Lab
2014	Lansbury	Shiria	Khatun	Lab
2015	Stepney Green	Sabina	Akthar	Lab

(Full list in Appendix)

15

Discussion

The growing presence of Bangladeshi women candidates—across multiple parties—demonstrates a shift in communal attitudes toward gender and leadership. Their participation wasn't solely measured by electoral victory, but by the widening scope of representation and influence in council decisions and public debate.

Conclusion

This chapter documents not just the inclusion of women in the political process, but their impact as agents of change. The legacy of early pioneers is now visible in the number of wards contested and the acceptance of women as both electoral contenders and community leaders.

Chapter 3

From Local Resolve to National Representation

This chapter highlight the significance of Rushanara Ali's election as the first Bangladeshi MP and what it meant for the Tower Hamlets community politically, culturally, and emotionally.

Abstract

This chapter examines the community's campaign for national representation culminating in the election of Rushanara Ali as the first British Bangladeshi MP in 2010. It explores the collective aspirations, electoral strategies, and the symbolic shift from local activism to parliamentary presence.

Keywords

Rushanara Ali, Bangladeshi MP, Tower Hamlets, national politics, representation

Introduction

The election of Rushanara Ali to Parliament in 2010 was a historic milestone not just for Tower Hamlets, but for Britain. It marked the first time a woman of Bangladeshi heritage occupied a seat in the House of Commons, representing Bethnal Green and Bow.

Body

3.1 Campaign Dynamics

- The selection process sparked intense interest within the local Bangladeshi community.
- Ali's candidacy reflected a desire to merge mainstream politics with local identity.

3.2 Identity & Expectations

- Her success was viewed as a collective breakthrough.
- Community voices saw her election as the "arrival" of Bangladeshis in national politics.

"We wanted someone who didn't just look like us—but understood us." — Tower Hamlets community leader

3.3 Election Data

- The 2010 general election featured multiple Bangladeshi candidates across parties.
- Concerns over vote-splitting and internal rivalry played out in the margins.

Table 3.1: MP Candidates (2010)

Name	Party	Bangladeshi Heritage
Rushanara Ali	Labour	Yes
Other candidates	Various	Yes / No

Discussion

Rushanara Ali's election triggered national media interest and community celebration, but also internal critiques about elitism, religious affiliations, and gatekeeping. This revealed tensions between symbolic representation and substantive responsiveness.

Conclusion

Ali's ascent represents both a triumph and a turning point—a marker of inclusion into British parliamentary democracy, and a signal that national politics could no longer ignore the voices of Tower Hamlets. Her victory elevated local activism into national relevance and laid the groundwork for future political inclusion.

Chapter 4

The Politics of Belonging

Abstract

This chapter explores how British Bangladeshi political identity evolved alongside party affiliation and borough demographics in Tower Hamlets. It investigates the tension between community loyalty and institutional allegiance, probing whether candidates represented party interests or served as cultural custodians.

Keywords

Representation, belonging, party politics, community identity, Tower Hamlets

Introduction

Political affiliation within the British Bangladeshi community has often been a negotiation between principles and practicalities. While Labour dominated the early decades, parties like Respect, Tower Hamlets First (THF), and independents challenged traditional allegiances. This chapter examines whether politicians were driven by party mandates or by deep-rooted cultural belonging.

Body

4.1 Labour's Evolution

- Labour regained trust post-1978 but faced backlash around 2006–2010 due to internal rifts and accusations of tokenism.

- Councillors who began with Labour often shifted to new platforms like THF or Respect when local priorities were unmet.

4.2 Respect & THF Surge

- Respect offered an anti-establishment narrative attractive to disillusioned voters.
- THF capitalised on local identity politics, promising community-first governance.

4.3 Independent Identity

- A growing number of Bangladeshi candidates stood as independents to reflect specific local concerns and avoid national party constraints.
- Independence often served as both a protest and a strategic manoeuvre following intra-party disputes.

4.4 Electoral Breakdown

Table 4.1: Party Representation by Councillors (1982–2016)

Party	Candidates	Elected
Labour	168	127
Tower Hamlets First	39	18
Respect	72	14
Liberal Democrats	92	11
Conservatives	82	1
Independent	49	3

Discussion

Many councillors were seen as "community ambassadors" first, and party agents second. This duality shaped voting behaviour, media perception, and career trajectories. The recurring question from voters—*"Are they party-led or community-led?"*—reflected deeper anxieties about representation and authenticity.

"We didn't vote for a party. We voted for someone who grew up around us." — Resident, Whitechapel

Conclusion

Political allegiance in Tower Hamlets among British Bangladeshis was never static—it evolved alongside boundary changes, leadership struggles, and community needs. The politics of belonging underscored every candidacy, forming the emotional backbone of local democracy

Chapter 5

Public Duty or Political Career?

Abstract

This chapter investigates the motivations behind electoral participation among British Bangladeshi councillors in Tower Hamlets, analysing whether political involvement was rooted in community service or personal advancement. Drawing from interviews, electoral data, and council allowance records, it explores a complex interplay between duty and ambition.

Keywords

Civic duty, political careerism, allowances, councillor motivation, British Bangladeshis

Introduction

The question of why individuals enter politics is particularly potent within communities historically marginalised from power. In Tower Hamlets, British Bangladeshi councillors have occupied an increasing number of seats since 1982. This chapter probes whether their motivation stemmed from service to their community—or from personal career development bolstered by the platform of council politics.

Body

5.1 Councillor Allowances and Incentives

- By the early 2000s, standard councillor allowances increased, with leadership roles receiving significant supplements.

- Analysis of borough records shows that income from council roles became a sustainable wage, sometimes exceeding median borough salaries.

Table 5.1: Example Councillor Allowance Brackets (2002–2014)

Position	Annual Allowance (Approx.)
Basic Councillor	£9,000–£12,000
Cabinet Member	£20,000–£25,000
Council Leader	£30,000–£60,000

(Sourced from borough transparency reports)

5.2 Interview Reflections

"Some people saw council work as an extension of their activism. Others saw it as a pathway into power, prestige, or even parliamentary opportunity." — *Interviewee, Stepney Green*

- Motivations ranged from housing and community projects to party affiliation and self-branding.
- A notable subset viewed council work as a stepping stone to higher office or career diversification

5.3 Electoral Strategy and Career Progression

- A handful of councillors shifted wards over time, tactically contesting seats where electoral likelihood was highest.
- Notable trends include former Labour councillors running as independents or under THF after party disputes, often retaining loyal voter bases.

Discussion

The duality of motive—community service vs. career progression—is not unique to Tower Hamlets. However, the rapid ascent of British Bangladeshi councillors, paired with intra-community scrutiny, made these dynamics more pronounced.

Political legitimacy often hinged on visibility, engagement, and delivery of council services. Yet behind closed doors, party power-broking, media relations, and reputational management shaped councillor trajectories.

Conclusion

The decision to enter politics among Bangladeshi councillors in Tower Hamlets emerged from layered motives: public duty, community identity, and strategic careerism. Understanding these motivations is crucial to evaluating both the successes and tensions within community representation.

Chapter 6

Discontent and Scrutiny

Abstract

This chapter investigates periods of political turbulence, media attention, and internal party disputes involving Bangladeshi councillors and representatives in Tower Hamlets. It examines how scrutiny—external and internal—shaped leadership decisions, community trust, and electoral outcomes.

Keywords

Media scrutiny, internal conflict, party disputes, leadership breakdown, Tower Hamlets

Introduction

As visibility grew, so did vulnerability. Between 2006 and 2014, Tower Hamlets became a focal point of national media coverage—not only for its demographic uniqueness but also for intense political infighting, allegations of misconduct, and controversial leadership shifts. For Bangladeshi politicians, this brought both prominence and pressure.

Body

6.1 Internal Party Conflicts

- Key splits within Labour and Respect caused reconfigurations of leadership and strategy.
- Councillors defected, formed new alliances, and challenged existing party mandates.

6.2 Media Allegations and Coverage

- Publications like *East London Advertiser* and *East End Life* began documenting internal disputes, financial controversies, and personality clashes.
- Some councillors were portrayed as hyper-local populists, others as party loyalists under siege.

"The media turned council chambers into coliseums. Every misstep was magnified." — Council officer, interview

6.3 Community Reaction

- Tensions between political factions often spilled into mosques, community centres, and local business circles.
- Grassroots disillusionment rose, particularly among older voters who had supported early pioneers.

6.4 Leadership Challenges

- Investigations into council governance—especially during THF's rise—resulted in legal reviews and a wave of resignations.

Table 6.1: Summary of Notable Leadership Turbulence (2006–2014)

Year	Incident Summary	Impact
2006	Respect–Labour fallout	Councillor shifts and media interest
2010	Allegations of financial mismanagement	External audits and public criticism
2014	Election result annulment inquiries	Legal and electoral scrutiny escalated

Discussion

Discontent within Tower Hamlets wasn't just political—it was communal. The entanglement of personal ambition, ideological disputes, and media influence produced an atmosphere of persistent scrutiny. For many Bangladeshi councillors, managing visibility became as crucial as enacting policy.

Conclusion

This chapter reflects on a defining tension in Tower Hamlets history: that between the promise of representation and the pitfalls of political exposure. Navigating scrutiny required not just resilience, but strategic reinvention.

Chapter 7

2010 – Triumph and Turmoil

Abstract

This chapter dissects the pivotal 2010 electoral cycle in Tower Hamlets, marked by a dual climax: the historic election of Rushanara Ali as the first Bangladeshi MP and the highly charged local council elections. It explores candidate dynamics, party fragmentation, voter mobilisation, and the emotional highs and lows experienced within the British Bangladeshi electorate.

Keywords

2010 election, Rushanara Ali, Tower Hamlets, council elections, political fragmentation, diaspora mobilisation

Introduction

The 2010 elections represented both a political zenith and a crucible for the British Bangladeshi community in Tower Hamlets. While the election of Rushanara Ali symbolised national integration, the local council races exposed fractures—within parties, families, and ideologies. This duality defined the moment as both celebration and conflict.

Body

7.1 The National Win

- Rushanara Ali's victory in Bethnal Green and Bow brought Tower Hamlets national visibility.

- The win was lauded as a "generational breakthrough" for representation in Parliament.

"It wasn't just her win—it was ours." — Comment from community gathering, 2010

7.2 Local Council Battles

- Council elections saw unprecedented Bangladeshi participation across multiple parties and independent platforms.
- Respect, Labour, THF, Lib Dems, and independents flooded the ballot.

Table 7.1: Snapshot – Candidate Count by Party (Tower Hamlets 2010)

Party	Bangladeshi Candidates	Overall Seats Contested
Labour	30+	50+
Respect	18	40+
THF (pre-launch)	9	15+
Independents	21	—
Lib Dems	11	—
Conservative	4	—

(Full data in Appendix)

7.3 Community Sentiment

- Simultaneous pride in MP victory and disillusionment with local politics.

- Allegations of vote-splitting, nepotism, and strategic fielding became common.

7.4 Electoral Fallout

- Internal party tensions intensified post-election, particularly in Labour and Respect.
- Councillors began shifting allegiances, laying groundwork for new party formations in 2014.

Discussion

The year 2010 exemplified the complexity of political maturity. While one part of the community achieved national acclaim, another faced fragmentation. For Bangladeshi voters in Tower Hamlets, these elections embodied both forward motion and internal reckoning.

Conclusion

The dual elections of 2010 stand as a momentous chapter in British Bangladeshi political history. They brought visibility, vulnerability, and transformation—setting in motion trends that would reshape the borough's political map for years to come.

Chapter 8

Community in Motion

Abstract

This chapter charts the emergence of community-driven political organisations in Tower Hamlets, particularly the formation of Tower Hamlets First (THF) and other grassroots platforms. It investigates how British Bangladeshis shifted from participation within established parties to the creation of political vehicles designed to reflect local identity, frustrations, and aspirations.

Keywords

Tower Hamlets First, grassroots mobilisation, party formation, diaspora politics, community-driven leadership

Introduction

Following years of disillusionment with mainstream party structures, several councillors and community activists broke away to form Tower Hamlets-specific political entities. Most notable was the rise of Tower Hamlets First (THF), a party that promised direct local representation unmediated by national politics. This chapter documents the conditions, decisions, and consequences of this community-led political mobilisation.

Body

8.1 Origins of THF

- Created in 2013–14 by former Labour affiliates dissatisfied with internal dynamics.

- Aimed to centre Bengali voices in policy decisions, housing, education, and public resource allocation.
- THF positioned itself as a party of the borough, not Westminster.

"We needed a party that spoke our language—literally and politically." — THF founding member

8.2 Other Community Platforms

- Respect, People's Alliance, and independents also drew support from disillusioned voters.
- These movements often emerged from youth organisations, mosques, and family networks.
- • Political diversity within the British Bangladeshi community broadened the electoral field, though not without internal tension

8.3 Candidate Surge

- 2014 council elections saw THF field dozens of candidates in nearly every ward.
- High levels of voter engagement were matched by intense political rivalries.

Table 8.1: Tower Hamlets First Candidate Summary (2014)

Ward	THF Candidates	Elected
Bethnal Green	3	2
Stepney Green	2	2
Whitechapel	3	3
Mile End	4	2

(Full breakdown in Appendix)

Discussion

The success of THF reflected both a strategic void and a community yearning to reclaim agency. However, concerns quickly arose around transparency, internal democracy, and media framing. Critics accused THF of operating through clan networks and opaque funding.

"It was power to the people—but which people?" — Commentator, East London Advertiser

Despite this, THF's brief dominance in the council marked a paradigm shift in local power—away from legacy parties and toward borough-specific leadership.

Conclusion

Community-led political formations like THF showed that representation in Tower Hamlets could evolve beyond the bounds of national affiliation. While their rise was not without controversy, they confirmed a truth long felt by residents: politics here is local, emotional, and deeply rooted in cultural identity.

Chapter 9

Behind the Ballot

Abstract

This chapter analyzes the electoral behavior and identity-driven voting trends among British Bangladeshis in Tower Hamlets. It focuses on cultural loyalties, strategic candidacies, and the sociopolitical factors that influenced ballot outcomes between 1982 and 2016.

Keywords

Voting patterns, Bangladeshi electorate, identity politics, Tower Hamlets, candidate strategy

Introduction

Ballots are more than ticks in a box—they're expressions of trust, memory, and belonging. In Tower Hamlets, voting behavior among British Bangladeshis has often reflected familial ties, cultural familiarity, and symbolic representation as much as policy platforms. This chapter dives beneath the surface of the borough's elections to understand what voters really saw when they looked at a ballot.

Body

9.1 Loyalty and Legacy

- Many voters exhibited longstanding loyalty to councillors or families with deep community roots.

- First-generation voters were influenced by personal interactions, mosque affiliations, and social networks.

"I knew his father. That's why I vote for him." — Resident, Limehouse

9.2 Strategic Candidate Placement

- Parties fielded Bangladeshi candidates strategically in wards with high ethnic concentrations.
- Dual candidacies across adjacent wards became common in the 2000s.

Table 9.1: Candidate Saturation by Ward (Sample: 2014)

Ward	Total Candidates	Bangladeshi Candidates	Dominant Party
Shadwell	15	11	THF/Labour
Whitechapel	14	10	THF
Bethnal Green	12	8	Labour

(Full breakdown in Appendix)

9.3 Generational Divide

- Older voters prioritized community service and personal relationships.
- Younger voters leaned toward digital outreach, issue-based campaigning, and broader party narratives.

9.4 Electoral Turnouts

- Bangladeshi turnout rates were often higher than borough averages, especially in key wards.

- However, apathy increased during years of internal party disputes and councillor controversies.

Discussion

Voting behavior in Tower Hamlets cannot be divorced from cultural and emotional context. Rather than pure party loyalty, ballots reflected a hybrid of trust, identity, and political practicality. Campaign materials, candidate surnames, and ward reputation all factored into electoral outcomes.

Conclusion

Understanding the Bangladeshi vote in Tower Hamlets requires more than tallying results—it demands attention to history, kinship, visibility, and reputation. The ballot became a communal language through which voters chose not just councillors, but symbols of themselves.

Chapter 10

Redrawing the Map

Abstract

This chapter explores the impact of boundary changes within Tower Hamlets and their strategic implications for political representation. It analyzes how ward restructuring affected party fielding, Bangladeshi candidate placement, and voter behaviour from 2002 to 2014.

Keywords

Ward boundaries, electoral geography, representation, Tower Hamlets, candidate strategy

Introduction

Electoral geography in Tower Hamlets has never been static. As the borough evolved demographically and administratively, the Local Government Boundary Commission for England (LGBCE) undertook periodic revisions to ensure balanced representation and effective governance. These boundary changes created new wards, merged old ones, and altered political landscapes. For the British Bangladeshi community, these shifts brought both opportunities and challenges in maintaining visibility, influence, and voter connection.

Body

10.1 The Mechanics of Redistricting

- Implemented by the Local Government Boundary Commission for England (LGBCE)
- Goals included balancing population numbers per councillor, modernising ward identities, and aligning administrative functions.

10.2 Ward Transformations

- 2002 reforms introduced new wards such as *Mile End East, Bethnal Green North, Blackwall & Cubitt Town*
- 2014 saw further refinements, with *Stepney Green* carved out and new delineations for *Canary Wharf, Poplar, Lansbury*
- These changes required parties to reassess fielding strategies and community engagement tactics.

Table 10.1: Ward Changes and Effects on Candidate Placement

Original Ward	New Configuration	Effect on Bangladeshi Representation
Limehouse	Split between 2 wards	More candidates fielded
Spitalfields	Became Spitalfields & Banglatown	Identity-centric fielding strategy
Mile End	Divided into East/West	Strategic THF fielding

(Full mapping in Appendix)

10.3 Strategic Adjustments by Parties

- Labour and THF fielded candidates in newly drawn wards where demographics suggested potential support.
- Candidates with strong personal followings were relocated to "safer" zones post-boundary change.

- Ethnic and religious community hubs heavily influenced where candidates were deployed.

10.4 Voter Behaviour Post-Boundary Reform

- Initial confusion among voters regarding ward names and polling station locations was widespread.
- Despite geographical changes, cultural familiarity, councillor reputation, and communal loyalty remained key drivers of voter choice.

Discussion

Redistricting can dilute or amplify representation. For British Bangladeshis in Tower Hamlets, it became a test of political adaptability. While parties recalibrated, many voters remained loyal to individuals rather than adjusted maps.

"We didn't vote by boundary—we voted by reputation." — Resident, Bow East

The strategic use of boundary shifts—particularly by THF— demonstrated a growing sophistication in borough-level political organisation.

Conclusion

Boundary changes in Tower Hamlets altered electoral landscapes, but not community identity. Representation remained centred on cultural familiarity and candidate visibility, showing that even in redrawn maps, the heart of politics stayed constant.

Chapter 11

Roots and Representation

Abstract

This chapter maps the ancestral and regional origins of British Bangladeshi councillors in Tower Hamlets, exploring how connections to districts such as Sylhet, Sunamganj, Moulvibazar, Hobiganj, and Dhaka influenced political identity, community trust, and representation. It reveals how the politics of diaspora entwined with village lineage and familial heritage.

Keywords

Zila mapping, Sylhet, Bangladeshi diaspora, political identity, cultural heritage, Tower Hamlets

Introduction

In Tower Hamlets, political representation among British Bangladeshis has long been shaped not only by party affiliation and policy but also by ancestral roots. District origin—known as *zila*—plays a quiet but powerful role in how trust is formed, votes are cast, and candidates are seen. This chapter looks at how lineage from Sylhet and surrounding areas factored into the borough's political tapestry.

Body

11.1 The Sylheti Majority

- Over 80% of Bangladeshi councillors in Tower Hamlets traced their roots to Sylhet.

41

- This common origin created tight informal networks and shared linguistic and cultural cues among voters and candidates.

11.2 District Distribution

- Specific towns and villages were disproportionately represented:

- **Sunamganj**: High representation in Shadwell and Spitalfields
- **Moulvibazar**: Candidate clusters in Mile End and Limehouse
- **Hobiganj**: Historical roots among early councillors from the 1980s
- **Dhaka**: Smaller but notable presence, often tied to independent candidacies

Table 11.1: Sample Zila Origins of Councillors

Councillor Name	Ward	District (Zila)
Md Ashik Ali	St Katharine's	Hobiganj
Shiria Khatun	Lansbury	Sylhet (Osmani Nagar)
Rabina Khan	Shadwell	Sunamganj
Abdul Mukit Chunu MBE	Weavers	Sylhet
Lutfur Rahman	Spitalfields	Moulvibazar

(Full mapping in Appendix)

11.2 Electoral Impact

- Voters often felt a stronger connection to candidates from their own district.

- Campaign teams leveraged these connections, appealing directly to zila-specific networks and community leaders.
- Ward-level outcomes occasionally reflected zila distribution patterns, especially where multiple candidates from similar origins competed.

11.3 Symbolism and Continuity

- For elders who arrived in the UK during the 1970s and 1980s, seeing a councillor from their village or thana (subdistrict) held deep emotional significance.
- Councillors sometimes referenced their district in campaign literature, speeches, or community gatherings to reinforce shared heritage.

"He's one of ours—from Osmani Nagar." — Resident, Weavers Ward

"He's from our village. Of course we support him." — Resident, Stepney Green

11.4 Critiques of Zila Politics

- Some community members viewed zila-based loyalty as exclusionary or outdated.
- In later elections, younger voters leaned more toward issue-based platforms than regional allegiances.

Discussion

Zila mapping reveals an invisible layer of representation: the heritage-based bonds that shaped candidacy, trust, and local leadership. While this form of identity politics helped create unity, it also risked factionalism and favoritism.

Still, lineage remained a source of pride, bonding, and legitimacy—especially among first-generation migrants who saw their councillors as extensions of home.

Conclusion

Roots mattered. In Tower Hamlets, the politics of representation ran alongside the rivers and fields of Sylhet. Councillors didn't just carry party cards—they carried ancestral echoes. This chapter affirms how migration, memory, and identity created a mosaic of political belonging—and how the Bangladeshi map quietly redrew the British one.

Chapter 12

The Numbers Tell Stories (Polished Version)

Abstract

This chapter presents a statistical overview of British Bangladeshi political participation in Tower Hamlets between 1982 and 2016. Drawing on ward-level data, candidate outcomes, and party affiliations, it maps the numerical landscape behind representation, highlighting patterns, anomalies, and trends across decades.

Keywords

Electoral data, Bangladeshi councillors, Tower Hamlets, political trends, representation statistics

Introduction

While stories and interviews offer texture, statistics reveal structure. Behind every ballot and campaign leaflet, numbers tell stories—about success, exclusion, loyalty, and change. This chapter aggregates election data over thirty-four years, focusing on British Bangladeshi candidates, their party affiliations, and their success rates across Tower Hamlets. The aim: to show not just who won, but what these outcomes suggest about the community's political evolution.

Body

12.1 Councillor Count by Year

- British Bangladeshi representation grew steadily from 2 councillors in 1982 to over 20 in peak years by the 2010s.
- Significant jumps occurred after boundary reforms and the emergence of Tower Hamlets First.

Table 12.1: Bangladeshi Councillors Elected by Year

Year	Elected Councillors	Total Seats	Representation %
1982	2	50	4%
1994	6	50	12%
2006	12	51	23%
2010	21	51	41%
2014	18	45	40%

12.2 Party Affiliation Trends

- Labour dominated early candidacies but saw defections to Respect and THF in later decades.
- Independent candidates rose particularly in years of internal party dispute.

Table 12.2: Bangladeshi Councillor Affiliation Summary (1982–2016)

Party	Total Councillors	% of All Bangladeshi Councillors
Labour	127	74%
THF	18	10%
Respect	14	8%
Liberal Democrats	11	6%

Party	Total Councillors	% of All Bangladeshi Councillors
Conservative	1	0.5%
Independent	3	1.5%

12.3 Gender Breakdown

- Female representation increased significantly post-2006, with candidates like Rabina Khan and Shiria Khatun entering council roles.
- Despite increased participation, women remained underrepresented compared to male counterparts.

12.4 Electoral Volatility

- Party switching, ward movement, and intra-community competition led to fluctuating vote shares.
- High competition sometimes split votes, resulting in unexpected losses.

Discussion

Data affirms what interviews suggested: that representation is not linear. The numbers reflect waves of mobilisation, backlash, and recalibration. The rise of independents, temporary dominance of THF, and consistent Labour presence show a community negotiating visibility in varied forms.

Conclusion

Statistics are not cold—they're carriers of memory. These numbers reveal growth, fracture, aspiration, and resilience. British Bangladeshi political participation in Tower Hamlets is not just a narrative—it's a measurable force.

Chapter 13

Legacy and Learning

Abstract

This final chapter reflects on the broader implications of British Bangladeshi political participation in Tower Hamlets. It considers the lessons learned, the legacy left behind, and the future possibilities for representation, activism, and community-led governance.

Keywords

Political legacy, British Bangladeshis, Tower Hamlets, civic learning, future representation

Introduction

The journey from marginalisation to representation in Tower Hamlets is not just a local story—it's a national lesson. Over three decades, British Bangladeshis transformed their presence from invisible to influential, reshaping the borough's political landscape and challenging assumptions about who governs and why. This chapter reflects on what that journey teaches us—and what it leaves behind.

Body

13.1 Lessons from the Archive

- Representation is earned, not gifted.
- Community mobilisation must be sustained beyond election cycles.
- Visibility without accountability risks eroding trust.

"We didn't just want seats—we wanted change." — Interviewee, Mile End

13.2 Enduring Legacy

- The councillors, candidates, and campaigners documented in *Pathfinder* leave behind more than statistics—they leave behind stories, strategies, and symbols.
- Their legacy is visible in youth organisations, civic forums, and the continued presence of Bangladeshi voices in local and national politics.

13.3 Future Possibilities

- As younger generations redefine identity and activism, new forms of representation will emerge.
- Digital platforms, intersectional movements, and transnational solidarity may shape the next chapter of political engagement.

Conclusion

Pathfinder is not just a chronicle—it's a compass. It points to where we've been, what we've learned, and where we might go next. The legacy of British Bangladeshi political participation in Tower Hamlets is one of resilience, reinvention, and relentless pursuit of voice. The learning continues.

Glossary

Bangladeshi Diaspora

The global community of individuals with ancestral origins in Bangladesh, including those settled in the UK since the 1950s–70s.

Boundary Commission

Short for the Local Government Boundary Commission for England (LGBCE); a statutory body that reviews and revises electoral ward boundaries for fair representation.

Civic Representation

The act of elected individuals serving public interests within local governance structures such as borough councils.

Electoral Ward

A local district within a borough used for council elections; wards are redrawn periodically to reflect population changes.

Lutfur Rahman

Bangladesh-born British politician and solicitor, currently serving his third term as the **directly elected Mayor of Tower Hamlets**. Initially elected in 2010, Rahman was removed from office in 2015 following a court ruling on electoral misconduct. After a five-year ban, he returned to politics and was **re-elected in May 2022** as leader of the **Aspire Party**, which also secured a majority on the council. His administration has since launched ambitious social programmes, including universal free school meals and expanded youth services.

Pathfinder Database

The internal archive of candidate lists, election outcomes, party affiliations, and interviews compiled by the author during research for *Pathfinder*.

Respect Party

A left-wing political party that gained support among ethnic minority voters in East London during the mid-2000s.

Sylhet Division

A northeastern administrative region of Bangladesh that includes the districts of Sylhet, Sunamganj, Habiganj, and Moulvibazar; origin of most British Bangladeshis in Tower Hamlets.

THF (Tower Hamlets First)

A locally formed political party established around 2013–14 to promote hyper-local governance and Bangladeshi community priorities.

Zila

A Bangladeshi term for "district"; used by the diaspora to denote ancestral home regions such as Sylhet or Sunamganj.

Appendices

Appendix A — Candidate Database (1982–2016)

A complete chronological list of British Bangladeshi council candidates (1982–2016), detailing wards, party affiliation, and election outcomes. A statistical backbone of representation trends.

- Complete list of British Bangladeshi candidates who stood in council elections across all wards
- Details include:

- Full Name
- Ward Contested
- Election Year
- Party Affiliation
- Outcome (Elected / Not Elected)

Note: Candidates with repeat appearances across election cycles are grouped chronologically for trend analysis.

Appendix B — Female Representation Timeline

An overview of Bangladeshi women in Tower Hamlets politics, highlighting key elections, parties, and outcomes. Complements Chapter 2's narrative on gender breakthroughs.

- Tabulated overview of Bangladeshi female candidates in Tower Hamlets
- Includes:

- Name
- Year(s) Stood

- Ward
- Party
- Electoral Outcome

This appendix complements Chapter 2's narrative on gender breakthroughs.

Appendix C — Zila Mapping of Councillors

A cross-reference of councillor names and their ancestral districts in Bangladesh (Sylhet, Sunamganj, Habiganj, Moulvibazar). Reveals how migration memory shaped electoral support.

- Cross-reference table showing councillor names and their ancestral district (Sylhet, Sunamganj, Moulvibazar, Habiganj)
- Columns:

- Councillor Name
- Ward
- Zila Origin
- Relevance in Voter Demographics

Based on oral interviews and campaign literature references. Confidentiality maintained where applicable.

Appendix D — Ward Boundary Reforms

Visual and tabular comparison of Tower Hamlets ward boundaries before and after the 2002 and 2014 changes. Shows how geography influenced candidate strategy and voter behaviour.

- Visual map + tabular comparison of ward boundaries before and after 2002 and 2014 reforms

- Includes:

- Old Ward vs New Ward Labels
- Year of Change
- Impact Summary (e.g. voter shift, candidate reallocation)

Supports Chapter 10's analysis on geography and representation.

Appendix E — Interview Sources and Transcripts

A curated list of anonymised interview participants with selected excerpts. Offers insight into motivation, identity, and political memory behind the ballot box.

- List of anonymised interviewees, role, year of interview, and theme discussed
- Selected excerpts (where permission granted) relevant to chapters on activism, careerism, and identity

Epilogue:

Politics, especially at the local level, is rarely preserved in monuments. It lives in flyers, in nameplates on council doors, in arguments after Friday prayers. It lives in memory—and in misremembering.

When I began this journey, I thought I was writing about councillors. Over time, I realised I was writing about us. About a people who arrived speaking in dialects, navigated bureaucracy with borrowed pens, and somehow, without maps or manuals, found their way into the civic engine room.

This book does not conclude the story of British Bangladeshi politics in Tower Hamlets—it simply pauses it. What began in Limehouse and Bow in the 1980s continues today in Whitechapel, Bethnal Green, and beyond, shaped by younger voices, new parties, and shifting coalitions of trust.

But one constant remains: representation, when claimed by those once dismissed, creates not just councillors—but confidence, continuity, and community.

As I look back over the decades—over doorsteps and manifestos, meetings and misunderstandings—I see more than victory and defeat. I see intention. I see hope inscribed in leaflets. I see footsteps echoing across alleys that once led to nowhere.

Tower Hamlets may change its boundaries, but the stories within remain. This book is just one attempt to hold them still for a moment.

Bibliography

Official Records and Reports

- **Tower Hamlets Borough Council.** *Council Minutes and Allowance Reports, 1982–2016.* Tower Hamlets Council Archive.
- **Local Government Boundary Commission for England.** *Tower Hamlets Ward Redistricting Reports.* LGBCE, 2002 and 2014.
- **Electoral Commission.** *Mayoral and Council Election Returns, Tower Hamlets.* UK Electoral Data Archive, 2010–2014.

Books and Academic Works

- Ahmed, Faruque. *Bengali Politics in Britain: Logic, Dynamics and Disharmony.* Creation, 2013.
- Akash, Mayar. *Tower Hamlets Bangladeshi Politicians' Reference Book 1982–2018.* Bangladeshi East End, MAPublisher, 2017.
- Alexander, Claire. *The Asian Gang: Ethnicity, Identity and Masculinity.* Berg Publishers, 2000.
- Anwar, Muhammad, and Pnina Werbner. *Black & Ethnic Leadership in Britain: The Cultural Dimensions of Political Action.* Routledge, 1991.
- Aziz, Suhail. *Breakthrough: Memoir of a British-Trained Bangladeshi.* The Book Guild Ltd, 2020.
- Eade, John, and David Garbin. *Community Politics and the Bangladeshi Diaspora.* Ashgate, 2006.
- Gardner, Katy. *Global Migrants, Local Lives: Travel and Transformation in Rural Bangladesh.* Oxford UP, 2001.
- Glynn, Sarah. *Class, Ethnicity and Religion in the Bengali East End: A Political History.* Manchester UP, 2017.

- Kalra, Virinder S., et al. *Diaspora and Hybridity.* Sage, 2005.

Interviews and Oral Histories
(Unpublished Personal Communications)

- Abbas, Helal Uddin. Personal meeting.
- Ali, Shahid. Telephone interview.
- Ali, Sunawhar. Telephone and text interviews.
- Choudhury, Jainal. Telephone and text interviews.
- Chunu, Abdul Mukit MBE. Home visit, meeting, and telephone interview.
- Huque, Md Nurul. Home visit.
- Jolal, Rajon Uddin. Home visit and telephone interview.
- Maxwell, Phil. Telephone interview.
- Miah, Ayas. Telephone interview.
- Mizan, Syed. Telephone interview.
- Pierre, Hugo. Telephone interview.
- Rahman, Akikur. Telephone interview.
- Uddin, Baroness. Text and phone interviews.

Journalism and Community Media

- Baynes, Mark. *Love Wapping.* www.lovewapping.org. Accessed 5 July 2019.
- Jeory, Ted. *Trial by Jeory.* www.trialbyjeory.com. Accessed 2012–2018.
- "Tower Hamlets Politics: Respect, Rahman, and Reform." *East London Advertiser*, 2006–2016.
- "The Rise and Fall of Tower Hamlets First." *The Guardian*, 25 Apr. 2015.

Web and Digital Sources

- "Tower Hamlets Council Election, 1986." *Wikipedia,* https://en.wikipedia.org/wiki/Tower_Hamlets_London_B orough_Council_election,_1986. Accessed 18 Jan. 2019.
- "Tower Hamlets Council Election, 1990." *Wikipedia,* https://en.wikipedia.org/wiki/Tower_Hamlets_London_B orough_Council_election,_1990. Accessed 18 Jan. 2019.
- "Lutfur Rahman Makes Comeback with New Political Party Tower Hamlets Together." *Love Wapping,* http://lovewapping.org/2017/01/lutfur-rahman-makes-comeback-with-new-political-party-tower-hamlets-together/. Accessed 5 July 2019.
- "Current Applications." *Electoral Commission,* https://www.electoralcommission.org.uk/i-am-a/party-or-campaigner/guidance-for-political-parties/pending-registration-applications/current-applications. Accessed 5 July 2019.
- "Altab Ali – The Fight for Equality." *Tower Hamlets Council,* https://www.towerhamlets.gov.uk/Documents/Leisure-and-culture/Events/Altab_Ali_The_Fight_for_Equality.pdf. Accessed 19 Apr. 2022.
- *Tower Hamlets Local History Library & Archives.* www.ideastore.co.uk/local-history
- *UK Government Data Service.* data.gov.uk

Sources Consulted

These materials were used to inform tone, context, and thematic direction across chapters. While not cited in the formal bibliography, they shaped insights, confirmed historical details, or provided firsthand reflection.

- **Internal Pathfinder Database.** Election tallies, candidate breakdowns, ward maps, and timeline markers compiled by the author over 8 years.
- **Community Flyers and Pamphlets.** Scanned materials distributed during the 1994, 2006, and 2014 elections by Labour, Respect, THF, and independents.
- **Mosque Noticeboards & Press Bulletins.** Announcements reviewed from Brick Lane Mosque, East London Mosque, and Darul Ummah over three electoral cycles.
- **Campaign WhatsApp Groups (Archived).** Informal conversations and candidate positioning discussions from 2014 and 2022 local elections.
- **Sylheti Oral Retellings.** Informal meetings and family storytelling sessions around candidate ancestry, zila origins, and political memory.

Endnotes

Specific contextual clarifications and archival footnotes referenced across chapters.

1. **Chapter 1**: The earliest British Bangladeshi councillors elected in the borough (1982) were from Limehouse and Bow. While official listings name 2, Pathfinder interviews suggest community awareness of 3.

2. **Chapter 5**: "Postcode loyalty" emerged as a term in campaign literature in the 1990s, often referring to cultural affiliation within specific estates.

3. **Chapter 10**: Boundary reform confusion in 2014 was exacerbated by late polling station communications—council minutes recorded 14 formal complaints by voters on the day.

4. **Chapter 11**: Zila mapping is approximate and based on oral accounts. District confirmation was not available for every councillor, but verified for 86% of names listed in Appendix C.

5. **Chapter 12**: Statistics exclude mayoral votes and refer only to council seat elections. Female candidate data was cross-checked with ElectionLeaflets.org and author's campaign archives.

6. **Glossary Entry – Lutfur Rahman**: His re-election in 2022 under the Aspire Party followed a five-year electoral ban. Aspire formed from remnants of THF and independents, gaining council majority.

Synopsis

From Sylhet to Spitalfields is a political and social chronicle that traces the journey of British Bangladeshis in Tower Hamlets from civic invisibility to elected representation. Drawing on archival data, electoral records, interviews, and community media, this work examines how identity, migration memory, party affiliation, and ward restructuring shaped the borough's political terrain over three decades.

Beginning with the first names on the ballot in 1982, the book delves into voting patterns, boundary reforms, generational divides, and the enduring influence of ancestral zila ties. It interrogates how candidates were selected, how trust was built, and how loyalty was brokered between local councils and community spaces.

With chapters focused on female political emergence, the rise and fall of Tower Hamlets First, and the numerical trajectories of representation, the book presents a multilayered account of how power was negotiated—and often contested—on the streets of East London.

Both academic and deeply personal, *From Sylhet to Spitalfields* serves as an archive of local memory and an invitation to future generations to trace not just votes, but voices.

www.ingramcontent.com/pod-product-compliance
Lightning Source LLC
Chambersburg PA
CBHW070954280326
41934CB00009B/2067